WILD BIRDS
AND OTHERS

Poems by Wendy Long

Photographs by Ron Sugiyama

Wild birds must be
caught young
and loved without
hesitation . . .
or they'll pass with death
and never know
of life.

CELESTIAL ARTS
Millbrae, California 94030

First Printing, October 1973
Library of Congress Card No.: 73-82533
ISBN 0-912310-32-4
Made in the United States of America

DEDICATION

They asked me who it was.
A painter Friend Chris
we met in yellow sun.
Chris it was who gave me butterflies
and paintings of the ocean.

So I wrote a song and a book
and we'll go to New England pretty soon
to live in a stone house
called Masada
and everybody will ask what it means.

Those who don't know me ask
and Chris is one who feels inside
before it's spoken and that's good.
Maybe that's where it begins.

It'd have to be yours, Chris. . .
a brass candlestick holder
and a Bethea
and a broken D string.
Nobody else'd understand.

Maybe they'll read.
It'll come a lot faster
and they'll grow
like California poppies
in Texas.

CONTENTS

Dear You:

Pretty soon
I'll start again
and meet you in
the strawberry patch.

We'll talk about it all
and where we've been
and where we'll go.
It's beautiful.

It'll take awhile,
and I hardly know
you, but we'll be friends.
It won't take long.

If you need me,
look inside.
I'm right here now,
and I love you.

WEN

1. THE FORGOTTEN

BETHEA

A little girl I knew once. She reminded me how to love.

Tiny girl of six—you be so young; so wise.
I met you only Saturday.
Your crooked smile reached to me
as if to say, "I love you: Please love me."

I will, Bethea. I'll love you more than you can fathom
because I too am hurting inside and understand your needs.
Besides, you're just a little child
who sees the whys of living and of dying.

Don't run, Bethea. Don't run away to cry
for I am but this close to you and would hold
you with the foster puppies
because you are so fragile and so gay.

Love with me now, my six year old friend.
I'll take you where I was so long ago.
We'll sit in swings—I'll push you high.

Up and up. Down and up.
It won't run out, Bethea.
The daylight won't run out.

And braid your hair like little girls do
and smile brightly . . . and fly so high.
You won't fall. I promise.

Little girls like you won't ever let go
of a magnificent flight through youth.

MICA

He taught me how to feel. Or have I taught him?

Mica told me that Somebody originated sunsets.
Just had enough faith and enough color and enough dedication
    and just attached it somehow to the sky.
Kinda like the final glory of a day,
    showing off its fullest array of music from the eye.

Mica was so old he seemed to know about those things.
He seemed to sense my need to know;
     so it was always the newness that he spilled into my cup.
He told me once that people got wrinkles just before they died.
It was the body shaking loose of its skin—like a rattler
     who disappeared from earth and came back in a change—
     like being born again.
Mica said the moon was Somebody's lamplight.
It was left hanging way up there to light the solar system
     and to guide us all once or twice a month in the mid of night
     without these fandangled contraptions Thomas Edison made.
Mica just had no patience for modern progress or conveniences.
He lived on berries and fresh cut vegetables
     which he traded for a goose every now and then.
Just fresh whole bread and raw fish
     and once in awhile a jug of cider.
Said Somebody put us here for what we could grow;
     not what we could process.
Mica must have known what he was talkin' about
     'cause he was spry and eager to outwalk you to the creek,
     and he must have been well into eighty.
Told me Somebody had been with him all these years
     telling him stories and telling him about the land
     and the right way to live.
Told me about when he was a kid and Somebody was always
     there to sit with him when the storms were bad
     and Who'd eat with him when he was alone.
Mica knew so much. I just wanted to hear it all.
Now he's gone, and I have become the shadow of his deliverance.
He belonged to that Somebody, and I guess I did too
     'cause now I'm walkin' from city to city and people are listening.
They're listening to Somebody else.
Somebody Mica lived for—a long time ago.

AND NOW
A WORD
FROM OUR
CREATOR:
"Love Your Neighbor"

TIME TO SAY

Time to say we nearly met
  Time to think how close
  our lives came—but not
   close enough.
How many are there at the touch
 who shy away
  with not a try
   nor friendly word?
It might have been
 a closer bond,
  but no one knew—
   or maybe no one tried.

FOLLOW ME MY SORRELS

The trust of freedom to follow arrival? It can be.

Follow, follow to the edge of summer.
    Follow me for one last gaze upon the rusted canyons.
My herds of sorrels and of bays—
    They chase me 'cross the earth, listening for another dream,
        but all is still.
My trust becomes imbedded in their deepest vein.
    I knew not of its worth until that day
    I looked behind and saw them coming after all.
Follow me, my sors, my children.
    I shall not deceive you; I shall not doubt.
We can ride the gifts of prophets
    who left this emptiness by mistake.
We can settle it and call it ours
    until the wrongers eat its heart.
By then it may not matter—for we shall be old—
And the sorrels will be grays, and the wind won't blow so loud.
Follow through another storm.
    The shelter sits beyond the hills.
      We'll hide for today and begin again tomorrow--
    to search for air and for what must surely be our only pride.
There is freedom in the wanderers.
They keep together always.
    They will not ever forsake the heritage.
    For in the open stands the only proof of value,
      and that is heritage.
My lovely children, follow me on this afternoon.
We need not commands nor punishments.
    We need but love and dedication.
      That is why we cannot lose.
We cannot ever lose, my darlings,
    for you shall follow me as it was meant.
I shall keep you free forever.
But when we reach the edge and are enclosed by wicked men,
    with no other escape and no better way,
    will you follow me to the rocks below?
I trust it will be so,
    for what is the wanderer without the far horizon?

2. BATTLE

We shall sing to be free,
But,
shall we die
still singing?

PANTHER

Panther stalks the rigid forest
one more day to
hunt for prey.
Tell us why it takes a lifetime
to fulfill.

Panthers cannot reply
except to continue to provide
and count the others he
uses for existence.

3. ONLY LOVE

What of the sun?
It rises in the east
and sets
in your eyes.

YOUR EYES

The moon has come.
Its meeting argues with your eyes
   knowing not which is the fairer.
I place judgement on them all
   for they belong to me and
      cannot be restricted.
And, I alas, must vote your eyes
   the more beautiful of the two.
For with the laggard reach of day
   oh, moon does break and fade away
      into the alien clouds.
And still with elapsing night
   your eyes do enlighten all the
      universe before me.
Such a spectacle cannot be
   denied this note of fond and
      total admiration.

LOVE

It floated 'cross the years beyond my sight, and so I feel.

What white swan glides for now into the mirror?
She floats away as leaves upon the water's edge
    in silent winds that touch the form
    but not the direction.
She seeks her level—watches for its lonely stare.
She scans the horizon for a dawn to come when
    dawn has long since been day.
She travels slowly, covering the wealth of rain
    in one brief stroke, reflecting both the beauty
    and sincerity of what she represents.
She follows blindly—with not a care of protruding
    limbs.
She uses not the sense of swans nor love, even—
    for she cannot see beyond her desires,
    and her desires must come first.
Ripples filter in the beam of light,
    tossing aside the souvenirs of love lost
    at no cost, and she forgets herself in happiness.
She taunts so many and flaunts her tail to tell
    them of what she has.
But touch, and she will bite.
She must be allowed that freedom to win and lose.
She must choose. She obeys only her own wants.
She is ignorant of discipline.
She never deceives, except to deceivers.
The great white swan at last shall continue.
So many wish to swim beside her,
    yet so few have learned the stroke.
Many have been hurt by her; many are her slaves,
    but if she is treated in tender truth,
    she can become as life's only companion.
For honest love is real.
And honest love can never die.

WOULD YOU CARRY MY CHILD?

If all the seasons melted together
    and turned their backs on us?
If no one ever knocked on your door
    again to court you because
    you became dedicated to me;
If redbuds filled our pastures,
    and apricot trees bloomed heartily,
    and the vegetables were plenty,
    and cattle were countless;
If dry winds came only after the flooding,
    and I built you a cabin of oak,
    and provided each new day
    with azelias and forget-me-nots;
If I blistered my hands on shovel and plow
    and, bent in years, created your every
        dream come true,
    and treated you as I would treat
        a newborne robin,
    and loved you as I would love
        the new-fallen snow,
    and respected you as I respect
        the coming of April;
Would you carry my child?

4. HOME AGAIN

Flowers on the desert.
Rainbows on the sea.
Bring them home to Mother.
Bring them home to me.

SAN FRANCISCO

Home one December, Oh, beautiful it was
long ago. Maybe next year.

The princess wore diamonds as she flowed so casually 'cross
    the lighted Bay.
Such an affair with her had I so long ago.
I wondered if I'd been forgotten as a tiny grain of sand
    through the crystal hour glass.
Then she smiled at me,
    her diamonds flashing as she breathed,
    her torso much too beautiful for such a youth as I.
For how could I deserve such radiance
    when my desertion is my cross,
    and my cross has been carried for too many years.
If I told her of the journey would she understand?
Would she take me back again to her bosom
    and let me try once more?
Even now, I must deny my power to stay,
    when I know it cannot be.
And I will watch her sparkling reflection as beads of hail
    'gainst the sun into a silver chalice.
Forgive me, dear lady, for my negligence.
Now I stare into your tender face and offer
    recollection of those months we shared.
You smile at me as a rhythmic splash of rubies
    to the marble floors of hours past.
It opens me and calls me back
    and forces me to admit before you
    that no other beauty could dare to stand beside you.
There is no other, fair princess.
There is no other, and there will not be
For when I go, I leave my soul at your feet to save for me
    and taunt me when I am away.
One day I shall return for it, I hope.
One day we'll begin again when life is not so bothersome
    with detail and with promise.

PAINTER FRIEND

Once I knew a child sweet,
  in yellow sun it was.
And she gave me butterflies
  and paintings of the Ocean.

When I saw into her face
little did I know of shadows
    bursting in gray.

When we met again in fall
    trees were crying in the rain
So we wove the golden leaves
    where children would remain.

If I think of yesterday
I can well remember feeling
    her warmest smile.

When we left the foggy dew
    we stood upon the bridge
tossing petals to the wind
    and waving from the ridge.

Tears were not my finest friends,
but they followed close behind me
    for many a day.

Soon the artist that I know
    will come again to see me.
We will find a house of stone
    along the eastern sea.

Then, perhaps, the words will come
and paintings of the ocean
    in one gentle year.

DOESN'T ANYBODY REMEMBER ME?

Doesn't anybody remember me here?
It seems as though my name is gone
    and face is just another cloud
    to a band of shredded geese.

It seems as though it'll never stop pouring.
January will be here soon with nobody
        to ask me why I'm so far away from the north.
I've searched a long time
        for somebody to recognize,
        but it seems that I'm not the only one to wander.
The wanderers never meet even strangers
        on the road—just shadows.
Shadows haven't time to stay.
Gutters fill and overflow.
The traffic slows a bit with people in the quiet
        and in the home.
Haven't seen home for nearly eight years
        except to visit
I often wonder if the pack will ever sleep to dust
        and the boots to time.
Cannot fathom a roof of my own—
        or a bed that doesn't have a pine cone in it—
        or a real oak table with a pot of lamb stew
        and hot pumpernickel—or an old cat named Ranger
        who says he doesn't care if I live or die,
        but I know he really does.
Can't imagine a fireplace with
        somebody there to talk to and to hold
        to share the dark with and listen to the stillness.
You can hear anything you want
        when you're with somebody,
        but you only hear yourself when you're alone.
Maybe one of these days
        I'll find a soul who could love this hulk.
We'd find a place on the map
        and head there to settle down and relax for a while.
Mama told me I was a dreamer.
I guess she was right,
        but some folks never even dream so maybe
        I'm further ahead of the crowd than I'd thought.

DRIFTER

Take me home, Drifter. Trail's gettin' battered
and the saddle squeaks beneath my weight.
Knees are passin' by, and soon we'll both be dead, Drifter,
if you don't get us home.

Been such a long way. Country bare and hot. . .wide apart
from other towns. And bones all bleached where cattle died.
We'll be lyin' close beside them unless the sun slows
down its awful smile. I've got to have water soon
and Drifter, are you makin' it okay?

They told me you were plum no good, never had a lick of
sense from the day you hit the ground.
So now I realize all those years of breakin' you were not
in vain, 'cause now you're all I've got, and
nobody'd get you from me, Drifter.

One day if we make it through, I'll be sure you get the
biggest spread a horse could ever roam on. . .with alfalfa
and grand old lakes and people will admire ya for
this last day. If we make it. We've got to make it.
You've got to take me home, Drifter.
The prairie is gainin' on us and the hope is losin'. . .
and I feel myself saggin' deeper into my own sweat and saddle.

Shoulda seen that saddle when it was brand new.
Sure was a pretty sight. Sure did make my friends sigh
deep and tell me I was crazy to spend so much for a big old
saddle and a little buckskin colt that had no brains.
So here we are, Drifter, you and me and an old saddle. . .
and buzzards overhead.
Lord, I ain't leavin' my flesh to a buzzard.

Keep on there Drifter, you fool horse.
You got to get us home again before we die.
Before we die, Drifter. We're gonna die.
We're gonna drop right here in the dirt and burn our
faces in the sun before the buzzards come.

Some folks been doin' that all their lives, you know.
Just layin' there in the dirt, wallerin' in sorrow. . .
Never tryin' to get up. Never tryin' to move.
Seems like nobody has any sense anymore.

Come on, Drifter, we got to keep on. We got to get home.
This old hat, I can't believe where it's been. Look at it
now. . .just hangin' on my head like an old dishrag.

Lord, how long will it be? Tried to sleep last night.
Covered my face in this old hat, breathed its leather smell.
Never saw the stars even. Just slept on through the night.

Now it's nearly night again. Drifter and me have been
on this trail nearly forever. I can't sleep, Drifter.
We've got to keep on. We've got to reach tomorrow.

Or water. Or ice. That's it. A huge lake with fish
and a waterfall. Coolness. Where you don't feel like you're
dyin' and you don't feel like anything matters. Just water.
But that was early yesterday. Seems like the prairie
never tasted water. . .never cared about it. . .
never offered it to anybody.

We've got to get home, Drifter.
The sky's flashin' in my head and I'm seein' things that
shouldn't be. And you're goin' lame.

If only man was as true to man as a horse is.
Rocks upturned here and there. . .
and ruts from some old wagon at the last rain
a hundred years ago.

Wonder if they'll ever find our bones?
Maybe I'll carve it in the saddle, who I am, and
where we're going.
Just me and a buckskin gelding named Drifter.

It was good. Never coulda had a better life.
Not perfect, but good.
Seems like it's been pretty long. . . Met a lot of good people,
and left them all behind.

Seems like I was born on the road. Always ready to move.
Always sayin' goodbye. Always had to have it my way.
Dumb fool. Shoulda settled down and lived a decent life. . .
had kids, read the scriptures.

Instead, here I am on a horse, driftin' again to who knows
where. And lost.
Take me home, Drifter. I'm so tired. I've got to sleep.
I've got to find some water and some food.
I've got to grain ya and put ya up in a giant stall
with all the water you can drink.

You're slippin', Drifter. You're slippin' fast and the
ground's comin' closer and the day's nearly gone.
Been wanderin' all my life. I was born wanderin'
and I'll die wanderin'.
Looks like it's time to rest now, Drifter.
Looks like the prairie's got us good.
Looks like we're nearly Home now, Friend.
Looks like we're nearly Home.

BREAD CRUMBS

Father, I am growing. Father, I am grown.
Father, will you weep for me when I am gone?

Indians tought me living. Or was it Mother?
Or was it just instinct?

BREAD CRUMBS

Lived with the Indians in 1967. The years were longer then, and there wasn't time for waste. Of course, when you live with Indians, you get to learn your own. You get to trust yourself when an old sway back mule dumps you in a heap of cactus and runs like hell across the prairie till all you can see is a cloud of red dust and a cannon you wish you had for one rotten mule.

Three days I walked. Three whole days and nothing to eat except grass and an occasional acorn. Lord, I don't know how the country lasted like it did. Some parts of it just weren't meant for civilized folks. And I swear I would have died for sure if some dumb-looking Indian hadn't showed up. He stood against the sun and I waited for his savage yell and the pain that should follow as he cut off my long brown hair. I was wishing Warner Brothers could catch this one. I'd go down in history with John Wayne and Gabby Hayes. But that old Indian just stood there staring at me like he'd never seen anything like me before. (And I don't guess he really had.) So anyway, I come to find out that the reservation was about two miles away and they'd have food, food, food, and water, water, water. That was for sure the longest three miles I'd ever walked. And when we arrived, everybody stared at me again like I was weird or something and he took me in this dug-out shelter and offered me a bowl of stew, I guess it was. But I'd have laid one hundred dollars down on it that it was that old mule that left me stranded. Toughest, rottenest meat I ever tasted. But when you're hungry, you just don't care.

Mom always told me, "Enjoy what you have now. For it may be gone tomorrow." So, I enjoyed that old mule, to the last piece of grissle. I like saying I lived with the Indians in 1967. It sounds real cool.

They taught me how to ride bareback and how to skin a deer and how to string a good bow . . . and how to squat in the bushes without getting your shoes wet. It sounds real cool, you know. But Mom knows about my stories and she used to say, "Now don't you go telling everybody those big stories. . . one day they'll see right through you and you'll be left alone to starve." Called all her great quotations my "bread crumbs." You know, little morsels of food that come in thoughts and digest throughout your innards, and you save them forever. Mom was a wise one for sure, but she still doesn't believe I lived with the Indians in '67.

I tell you, Mom, they had this old pickup truck, 1942 it was, and it traveled eleven miles per hour, full throttle. But it would climb trees and tear up fences. So one day we filled it full of screaming kids and drove them thirteen miles from home, let them all out, and left. They hollered at us till we couldn't even hear them anymore. And that night they trudged into camp just grumbling and groaning, and none of them said a word to any of us for three days straight. Silence is their greatest virtue. (There's a bread crumb for you, Mom.) It seems a pity to me that people have to live on that desert with nothing to do and I just can't see why the emptiest corner of land is so full of human bondage, but no one will water it or let it blossom. And, so they sit on their front porches and sing and drink, and dance sometimes. . . and that's *it.* Where have all the bread crumbs gone?

Somebody said the Indians are well taken care of. I trusted their word. . . and now I see that broken vows are prominent in the mouths of the rich and the eyes of the poor. Have that bread crumb on me, you rich slobs. Maybe if you'd choke on it once it'd open your mind. But, I guess I'm dreaming again. So, anyway, I sat by myself one evening and watched the sun go down. Indian children laughed and played, like the whites, but they'd become adults, like the blacks, and no one would ever hear their bread crumbs. . . except me. Maybe if I holler loud enough, they'll either listen, or they'll assassinate me.

I left the Indians in November. It was just starting to get cold and they were collecting wooden chairs and bed frames for their fires. That old truck sat there, sagging and weary with age, like the Indians. And I knew one day, while no one noticed, it would be too late. Too late, huh? When it's too late, what'll you do then? When it's too late for the red men it shall also be too late for you. Because, like the seasons change, and the flowers fade and die, we can live awhile without them, but pretty soon the balance lacks—then sways—then topples. And you shall be the first one to reach the *bottom* of the *heap!*

BLOSSOMS

Bound in orange string, the papers gather dust,
   waiting for a rusty bike and a ten-year-old to come.
It may be a long wait. . . ten-year-olds find circuses
   in the roads and steady jobs seem dismal.
The sidewalk is cracked.
In the air I catch the odor of freshly cut grass.
It carries me home where Daddy
   mows the lawn each Saturday.

Funny how one forgets until now. . .
    and it rushes by at bullet speed,
        allowing just a whiff, and then is gone.
Could there ever be a more appealing and colossal
    fragrance to the place or episode of life
        than that of bacon filling the woods?
I could die a glorious death with just that
    smoke surrounded about my cozy tent
And would I give my fortunes to be there now,
    to gather kindling and pine cones for the fire
        and for that iron pan that spits its black upon my white.
I might inhale the first breath of lemon as the knife
    refuses delay of its juicy interior. . .
and sip its curdled wine. . . yet no one is aware,
    I think, of timeless odors and gentle airs.
I might run forever, breathing deeply of the
    freshest earth following the freshest rains.
Why, tell me friend, have you smelled this richness,
    this fullest encounter with the soil?
        I trust you have not.
So let me take you next to the railroad tracks
    with creosote and tar.
Adventure and goose bumps clothe my ideas.
To be free to ride the box cars from
    Sacramento to St. Louis, and in between,
    to bask in civilization and in wilderness,
    knowing I am of neither; I am of my own.

I might return to Bolinas to whiff the ocean breezes
    as they carry salt and sand flakes over dunes
    to settle on the cheeks of lovers and of loners.
I want at last to rest beside the sugar pines.
I want to feel their strength upon my touch. . .
    to hear them whisper as the night winds beckon.

CAFFE TRIESTE
ESPRESSO
PIZZA PIE

LITTLE ITALY

Little Italy
a small cafe
in Texas
where we sat
one night.
We told jokes
and laughed a lot.
Shared spaghetti
and a salad. . .
and fought over
an olive.
Maybe we can
meet again
in the fall at
this same table.
We'll laugh then,
in joy, I hope.
For now,
we laugh
to hide the tears.

WINTER'S GULL

Winter's gull at
last has cried to sea,
calling for the sailor
who is far away
and the child lost
on a subway.
Hear his plea?
Oh yes, do we.
And echo, too,
our own refrain
to let them know
that we do
love them well. . .
and they be not
vacant and deserted.

ROLLER SKATES

I never roller skated when I was a child.
It wasn't that I didn't want to . . .
Little kids walked by, skates slung over their
shoulders, with bloody knees and skinned elbows.
I wasn't one to inflict pain upon myself,
and roller skates might have tried.
It wasn't that I was clumsy, either,
but, you see, at that time I was proudly
leading the life of a gallant, fierce,
coal-black stallion.
And gallant, fierce, coal-black stallions
don't wear roller skates.

GRASSHOPPER

A grasshopper tried to spit
    on me once.
Lucky I'm patient.

He might have surely drowned if
I had taken strong revenge.

CATERPILLARS

Caterpillars, yellow, orange, brown
   Wow. I could hold one forever. . .
Just watch it scurry
   'cross my fingers
   headed for who knows where.
So soft and delicate.
Oh yes, I do *love* caterpillars.
   Forever and ever.
I shall feel their skin
   against my cheek
and save them from the
   fate of a heavy boot.
But as much as I love
   these creatures and would protect
     their tents
   and hold them in my palm,
   why do they never
   fail to leave a tiny heap
   of greenness on my
   loving hand?

5. DIAMOND IN THE MUD

FOOLISH FRIENDS

Foolish friends, we call it that simply.
    We look at it that way, to stand in front on inane temptations.
Fools as we be are not torn by belonging, only remembering.
Fair and foolish friend of mine, we say the truth out loud,
    and circus clowns are painted, but they cry somewhere.
        Do you know of them?
Surely you must, surely you have seen them
    on stage, laughing in a bubble, and popping at the curtain's fall.
We are left behind, dizzy and curious.
    I've seen you before.
    I've seen you cry when tears were none.
        I've seen you fear when trials were of
            innocence, but the plea was guilty.
I love you, friend fool.
I see you naked in this dream,
    a child's body; a primitive sketch from artistic,
        trembling hands.
    Many dare not invade the fool's world.
    Many dare not face the covenant.
Many furnished purses, but no reward.
    Many, stricken and renowned to few, sat on
        the bleachers and tried to pray.
An apple seed began to grow, but no one noticed.
My golden fool, you will leave us soon. You will travel.
I am reluctant to set you free, though I have you not in actuality.
    Were you mine, then I would beg,
        but beggars have no jurisdiction.
We acquired wounds of plenty, felt their wrath,
    and found no dealer for their sale.
We ache for mercy, finding negation.

The crowd has faced the opposite shore to wave to their
    sailors who go off to sea.
We wave in silence. Yet, we cannot drown on destiny's reef.
Fools never drown. Perseverance is their fleet,
        and reliance is their anchor.
Fools bring forth immortal wisdom.
They have eaten clouds on a heated day when all was burned,
    and now their hearts are granite-firm, but feather-gentle.
Fools begin with continuity,
    clashing arms with doubtful men,
    challenging the sweat from seven centuries
            where people fought, and lost to self-defeat.
Fools do not end, you see. They know no lie, except in deceit.
        And those who dare deceive a fool will not
            retain the oath of timeful chances,
        nor catch hold of tomorrow's slippery wake.
My fool of fools, my friend of foolish desires,
    we have forsaken no one.
    We are not selfish,
        and if there was a place to sleep,
    we'd locate all the dynasty of one or two eras.
We'd quote the scriptures to the deaf.
    Perhaps they'd hear, perhaps not.
But, if we know already, and swear by
    all that's truth, that no grave error can interfere,
    then suffering is our cane,
        and our cane renews courage,
        and our courage is our foundation;
Foolish friends we be, and defy our fated courses,
    giving way to pleasantries in order
    to live and let others live.
In order to remain open to sensuality,
    I do forsake even my own doubts,
        for, I trust the first idea,
            and I have lost only rarely.

We shall continue weeping in silence,
for none must know our weakness.
Yet, we can extend the knowledge of these
    twenty-five years, and learn ourselves
        for their discretion.
I give you mine.
I accept yours.

    Fools are fools only to others.
We are fools of noble state, unaware of greed.
    Come with me, my faithful fool.
    Let's remain this way always,
        never to be captured by a faultless dream
            or a classic discovery.
We must remain our own, foolish as we may be,
    `But together, through the years,
        giving four hands instead of two,
    and two hearts instead of one.

LIFE

Fate is earthly. Death is not.
   Death is the seeker. Man is sought.
   Man is questionable, making his own decisions. . .
      yet insulted by his finality. . .
         and crawling for advice.
Man is winner. Man is loser.
   Life, the referee, and we, the audience.
      Thus, we play each role.
Roles are false. Roles are identical to facades,
   and facades create a rubbing pain that finds
      a corner and hibernates,
   thus, becoming a blister.
Blisters are on hands of farmers,
   heels of golfers,
     toes of hikers,
        and butts of lazy jackasses.
   Jackasses are common, they are in man.
      Man is whole to body, but not to spirit.

Spirit is the ghost that haunts his ignorance and taunts his pride.
   Pride is man's downfall. Pride takes over in the end,
      marring both the oaken home and oaken heart.
Hearts are keeping beat with routine, unless free.
   Routine is the atom bomb for rats and dogs and man.
   Routine is colorless, vague, and conqueror.
   Routine smiles sweetly at its captors.
      Captors cry in silence.
Silence rules the church, except on Sunday when it unites again
   with Routine, collecting vibrations of ten million
      muffled throats who cry in prayer. . . and
   apologize for not caring,
      and leaving fulfilled.

Church is free, yet empty.
Emptiness is at its ebb, it glides along the sand and never says
    a word, picking out the special shells and cockles and
        sleeping bodies.
Bodies are the grace of uneasy creations.
    They are tormented, mistreated, and discarded.
    They are the scars of lacking patience.
Patience is the answer, yet no one knows.
    Patience is the chilly air and distant horizon that
        called upon, and waited, and won.

Winning could be easy, given time.
        Time is forever. Time is not bought
        or stolen. Time belongs to no one,
            and to everyone.
Time can spare or share or dare or tear or wear,
    but it is not the chooser.
Choosers are the best, but hard to find.
    Choosers need not plead nor wail.
    Choosers know their quota, and they ripen.
Ripening is imperative,
    like patience, but who will wait?
Waiting takes a long time, and it is not easy.
    Waiting changes and matures, and is found on
        faces of no wrinkles.
Wrinkles are the rewards for what we are.

    We are our own images. What we are, appears one day
        upon our faces.
    Youth does not tell. Old age does.
Old age is the final lap. It takes us all.
        It is not choosy nor forceful.
    It knows its ability and its ultimate.
Old age is enemy to man
        Old age is kind or cruel. And its decision
        shows in the eye of the receiver.
        The receiver gains bounty from faith.
Faith surmounts sun and stars and universe.
            Faith begins hope. Hope begins life.
        Life begins man. And in it all,
    the circle traces the ascension of space and fertility.
Fertility provides compassion and recognition.
    It conceives no property except love, unless misused.

Fertility is the bud of language.
Language is the communicator.
Communication finds fault if language is broken
or tongues are paralyzed.
Communication controls love.
Love controls soul. Soul controls all.
Love takes place of soul, or else lost.
Love and soul united are totality, and are colorful.
Love is beginning. Love is strength.
Strength is compulsive, yet gentle.

It rules the ground, replacing only ash.
Ash is man when he is dead.
Dead is man when he is ash.
Man is ash when he lacks soul.
Soul is dead if it lacks man.
Man and soul and love provide perfection.
But, perfection must not be obtained, or all is lost.
Perfection needs advancement and courage.

Perfection demands fight. If lost, it is scar.
Scars blanket all. Scars are pain,
but pain is growth, and growth is power, and
power is explosive in the core of those who handle it well.
Power is soul. Power is man.
Man finds power in soul and power in love and power in man.
Death is traitor and pursuer, and judge.
But man who has soul, and all that goes,
can surpass death and ash and vengeance,
far beyond his own reach,
if only eyes are lifted.
If man did not look down,
it could never end.

AMERICA
COME
BACK TO
GOD
BUT AS THE DAYS OF NO'E
WERE, SO SHALL ALSO THE
COMING OF THE SUN ℀ OF
MAN BE

I'M DYING, PRAISE THE LORD ANYWAY

Cattle calls are softer, almost faded.
   I lay again in clover where the bees have been,
   where its honeys melt with summer. . .
      and I be a poor poet who sings of sadness, and of others.
I'm dying. Praise the Lord anyway.
I be too young to leave just boot prints
        in the moistened sand.
   My horses follow, with not a rope, the way God meant it. . .
      like planting seeds, and they grow,
         but you just don't know why.
My family's west. I don't see them much.
   I don't understand why we were woven as muslin,
      and now be frayed. . . but not apart.
      Hearts never separate. Only bodies.
I'm dying. But praise the Lord anyway.
Maybe Texas. I never lived there.
   Maybe I could start all over,
      find some land and build a promise.
      It could last. I know it could.

But could I? How long is there in a day?
　　So many times I have been bored and impatient with
　　　　daylight. Now it is all I have left.
I'm dying, you see, but praise the Lord anyway.
Knew a man once, not much to his outside.
　　But inside he was like the silver dollar in your jeans
　　　　when there's nothing else and you're all alone. . .
　　　　and you know there's a way, but you just don't know
　　　　　　how to use it, or if you should. . .
　　Or maybe you'd better toss it away before you spend it wrong.
So, I tossed him away, and I bled a lot,
　　　　and still do sometimes,
　　but then, I'm dying now, and praise the Lord anyway, I guess.
Got caught in a bad storm once or twice. Just sat there,
　　　　soaking wet and praying I wouldn't be sucked up
　　　　　　by some durned tornado. And I wasn't.
And I took off a hundred miles away to get out.
But you always remember those bad times
　　　　and when you see the clouds
　　forming, you hike up your collar and you look for shelter
　　and you get prepared to stand a little harder and you
　　　　wait till it's over and it usually is.

　　　　And it usually doesn't hurt, but then, I'm dying,
　　and storms aren't so important now,
　　　　but praise the Lord anyway.
Have this leather hat.
　　　　Picked it up in California a few years back.
Has grease and sweat on it,
　　and a lot of personality and it's mine.
　　I wouldn't trade it for a new stetson or a shotgun even.
Lost it once. Flew off my head
　　as I was riding this old gelding.

We must have chased it ten miles and found it in a creek.
     It's stiffer, but it's still mine and it's staying on me
          for good, even if I'm dying. Praise the Lord anyway,
               if He's listening. And don't forget about my hat.
It's just about time to move, I guess.
     You've all been everything a person could hope for.
You've caught me unprepared and
     I just can't find any words for saying what I feel.
So, I'll send you a line now and then
     and think of you when it's extra pretty outside.
I hope I've left you with a new bond and a new
          message. I want to be remembered without pain, so I better
               go, 'cause I'm dying now. But praise the Lord anyway.

POTATOES

Warm old wilted potatoes out there on my fire, cooking away,
    boiling away, to dead to really care.
Birds aren't singing much today,
    they know I don't need annoyance.
Mountain out there yonder, beyond this green tent.
    It keeps telling me to come on over and spend a few hours
       with it. I can't, mountain. I'm dying, mountain.
    Don't you see, mountain, I'm too weak to crawl.
I'd like to go, if I could. We have a lot in common.
    We'd get along fine, I reckon.
I'm proud and hard, and strong . . . and sensitive,
      like that mountain.
I didn't mean to hurt its feelings by staring there,
    'cept maybe it's understanding.
That old tree outside the tent is dropping pine cones
    all around me. Friend or enemy, I don't care, they're all
      the same to me. My feet are cold and tired and cut and
    blistered. Just like the rest of this tired old body.
    My time of dyin'.
Somebody's choppin' wood out there somewhere.
Man needs superiority, cuts up a tree, watches it fall.
    He's always cuttin', and watchin' things fall, 'cept himself.
Ants in here, crawlin' around, buggin' me,
    like a bunch of flies.
I can't sleep. I'm dead tired, in dead pain, and half-dead,
    and I still can't sleep.
Poor old potatoes, still smouldering on that hot fire.
Boilin' away their vitamins and strippin' their skins,
    marchin' 'em stark naked in front of the world.
Pain all runnin' up and down their bodies,
      and they gotta hide it and act brave, and bleed and die inside,
and tell no one about it, and just keep on boilin' until

they're soft and limp, and downright dead,
        but *dead,* I say. And then somebody'll eat them in peace
    and they'll be gone, but gone forever, and plum forgotten
unless they give somebody dysentary, and the people will hate
    the poor potato for making 'em sick, but how do the people
        know it was the potato? It mighta been their own saliva.
But that's too realistic and too humiliating,
    so the old leather people blame it on a dead potato.
Eases their minds, I reckon. . . and that's all they care about.

Wind's whippin' in and out this tent,
    and buggin' me, like the ants.
        Just knocked the axe over. That old wind's mad today. . .
            but stop takin' it out on me, wind. I'm doin' nothin'
                'cept dyin'. . . and that's no business of yours.
My feet are cold, and I'm too weak to find
        a pair of wool socks.
Hang on there, feet, if I can do it, so can you
Hairy old bee tryin' to get in here.
Go to hell, bee, I don't want you in here.
    My nose is bleeding again, but I don't sympathize.
    What do I care? Old nose gets too much attention.
Too much pain here now, nose.
    I've no strength to care about you.
    This old pack canvas I'm layin' on is strong, but strong.
Strong enough to be wrapped up and buried in.
        My mind's all shot to hell
    No transfusions, no morphine, no nothin'
'Cept me, and I'm not enough to keep me goin' for long.
I gotta get up somehow and rescue those potatoes.
    Gettin' soggy, I reckon. . . like me.
They tell me that Bear meat is no good
    So I take a bucket, and boil the meat three hours,
        stick in a rock, boil two more hours, and when the rock's done,
        you throw away the meat and eat the rock.
    Boy, just me here. . . me and my best friend, Pain.
I'm layin' back here in my refuge. Just checked my potatoes,
    and they're fightin' to keep hard mighty well.

So I'll give them a little longer,
    they can't hold out forever.
Silhouettes of pine branches on this tent's roof.
      They're itchin' to get in and bug me, I figure.
    You lose, pine tree.
      'Cause nobody else is comin' in here,
          'cept the wind.
    I don't want any company
When I die, I die alone.

SUN

Sun is immobilized in the leeward sky.
  It becomes oval, half-crushed by a cumbersome
    veil of pitch.
Oh Sun, why do you cry out in anguish?
Why do your piercing sobs vibrate the true atmosphere,
  calling us liars and deserters?
I kneel before you, Sir, disgusted and regretful;
  for I share your dismissal, and your reasons.
    I am torn inside, as a member of this civilization,
      though not an advocate.
I justify nothing of this outrage.
  And forgiveness could only prove worthless.
  They know not of their stupidity.
    What is left, fair Sun?
    We sleep at night. We sleep at day.
    We have no time for friends.

Therefore, you are ignored. And in this, we inherit the
    blackest doom, where crows stand out as ghosts
        against the flames of hell.
    Yet, even they shall drown in this defeat. . .
    and nothing can I do to interrupt the climax.
I have pleaded to you before this, on nine separate occasions,
        and you spoke of prosperity and prime.
    You laughed at my wit, and we mapped the poorest regions
        to a new and everlasting globe,
        that they would succeed.
We reminisced, and you rejoiced in the efforts
    of your smile, and the outcome.
But, I see you are gray. . . exhausted,
    and nearly a horizontal line.
    Your fullest capacity has liquefied,
        filling the lakes with melted butter,
        neither edible nor desirable.
Forgive us, Sun,
    for this deplorable act of selfish murder.
    Your gifts of foliage and warmth and compassion
        are cremated beneath a pile of sand,
        with no marker and no excuses.
It is too late for us now.
    You have dwindled too long,
        and they thought you were not earnest.

And now, at your bed of pale,
    I can send only a tear. . .
        my heart weeps blood for you,
    and I know I cannot change
        the world's filthy habits.
    And I know that your death will be
        their ultimate sacrifice.

Find another planet to protect, dear Sun,
    if you have the will. . .
        one with a shoulder to cry on
        and a mind that springs love.
This was a gamble.
    It was not you who lost, dear and desolate sun,
        it was mankind.

ENDLESS

You come to me, as if a child to this curious earth.
    You lean against a whittled staff to listen to my word.
I say to you in truth, as the dove says to its offspring,
        that all else which has real meaning, be simply and
        profoundly endless.
Endless be this night, with silver sequins on its sleeve.
    Endless be the kiss of eventide when swans disappear
    upon the lake in a million ripples of precious water.
Endless be a sacrifice and a dedication.
    It feasts upon beautiful souls, bringing to the
        surface, their very interior.
    It catches flight with golden cranes and whistles with the
        breezes of east.

Endless has no beginning, it has no end. It salutes the bleak and
    cluttered existence, a metamorphosis of color and softness.
It speaks every dialect and hears every invocation.
    It collects foreign coins, dropping them on the reef
        where they shimmer with the breakers and bury in the sand.
Endless knows the dusk of day, and puts it carefully to sleep.
    It is the song of summer and the maypole for children.
        Endless is sunlight against a smoky window,
            casting forth the pointed stars of God, perhaps,
        into the eyes of one.
Endless is forever. It stretches far beyond your faith, and mine.
            It streaks the heavens with blue,
                it reddens the robin's breast.
        It never judges. It only accompanies
And when you are lonely, endless brings to you
    a butterfly and a caterpillar, or a golden poppy from
        California, or salt spray or a yellow bee.
Endless reminds us of the forgotten miracles; of earthworms
        and hoot owls, of skunks and spinach and horse shoes.
    Endless is the quiet time, and a moment of prayer,
        and a letter from Mom, or a thought from God.
Endless be my only love. It shows me night and day,
    hard and soft. Endless rules my heart.
    All I see and all I know can have no bounds, and I am not
        shackled by it. Rather, I am endless to it.
I give my all to endlessness, and rejoice in my belief and
    in my spirit.
        Endless am I. Endless are you.
        Endless is God and beauty.
        What more does endless need?
Endless needs us, now and always.
Endlessness is endless, but some, maybe millions, will never
        know. And I pity them.

What we have now is *all*.
> With it, we shall retain the richest love, the truest
> honor, and the most worthy devotion.
Endless will not fail us, and we shall be forebearers of its
> weight.
> With this endless conquest, we shall now, and forever,
> be free.

TRAIN

In a southern railroad station I'm alone and facing noon.
Does it matter if I'm different?

I don't think so. I don't even think I'm different.
Old men hide behind their papers, chewing smelly tobacco,
searching for a subtle place to spit, besides the floor.
    It's always like this. Depots never differ.
Nearly two hours now, wasted day. Read magazines and wish
        Mom and Dad would call me home.
There's so much garbage on the streets and on the people.
Don't they know someone hurts in this world?
Don't they see beyond their cellophane fantasies?
Train's late again.
I'm so hungry. Just a baloney sandwich or a banana. . .
    or a friendly word from one who may not be stone deaf.
They bump up and down the aisles,
    pushing each other and grumbling. Doesn't anybody know me?
Can't anyone see that I'm real and in love with life?
    I guess not. People are in comas. God, why?
Look here, people. Wisteria. Beautiful wisteria.
    Do you see it? No, they turn away and
        crunch on chocolate bars and practice frowning.
All the other times I've sat here like this,
    nearly crying for what there isn't. And the trains
        come and go, surrendering mummies to these tombs.
I've just got to go and find a laugh or a tear,
            or someone who dwells in others.
Little kids are writing on the walls, dirty words I've known
    a long time. Doesn't anybody care?
Damn train. Always late, triggering a violent blow from
        society to a wanderer such as myself.
Relax now. Find a tune and whistle till the train comes in.
I was young once. Had it all. Still do.
    But got to hold it in my hands.
        People just don't have it anymore.
Where are you going, you faceless creeps?
Running to each other and falling off the edge of another
novel. Following the heads in front, no left, no right. .
        Should I ignore it all? Yes, for now.
The train has come to take me to another city of empty names.
    I'll preach this smile. . . maybe it
        will gain response.

DUCKS

Seclusion. We all be strangers to this seclusion.
Someone left it here, quite by accident. We share it
with no other clan, and no other language.

The Greeks spoke of seclusion as the Favor of God Himself. . .
    So would it then be here for such a modest time?
Its shores are uncluttered with the wasteful touch of humans.
What a rarity. There be but one sound besides the wind,
    eleven tiny ducks are marching down the bank,
        perfect cadence, almost. . . and perfect harmony.
They know no spear, no crooked tongue, no jagged tooth.
They glide into the shallow glimmer,
    floating off, a tiny fleet of cotton feathers, oblivious of me.
Is this the perfect bliss? Is this where God began His work
    and cradles the toys which He invented?
Is this the established peace which was to be our ground?
    Or dare I question it out loud?
        It must be so. . . for as the furnace warms
    this place, it also collects each object.
As in a kaleidoscope, exaggerating the perspectives,
    and spreading them everywhere as honey over jewels.
Ducks are innocent of hardness.
    They are fluffy buoys, bouncing over the waves,
        diving through the glitter for pollywogs. . .
    and babbling to each other as if nothing is said.
But, perhaps their babble is the true capacity above all else. . .
    and they be even more skilled than I,
        since I do not apprehend their words.
They swim the depths and scan the shores,
    as if they own it all, but are too humble to admit to it.
If this be God's, then surely I am richer
    just in seeing what He holds.
This is the focal point of everything. . .
    the warm, the soft, the gentle, the patient,
        the all-knowing, the all-caring. . . the epitome of God.
This is where He rests His head and cleans His feet.
This is where God begins each new day and each night, where
            He breathes and smiles.
Eleven white ducks return to shore, single-file and carefree. . .
    waddling into the clearing and are gone until tomorrow.
I hear them babble in the distance, wondering if they know of God.
Surely they must . . . or they would not be so exquisite.

TIMMY

A little boy who built a sand castle and fell in it.

Timmy playing on the beach.
I know he's Timmy—his mother called.
He chews on leaves and digs such tiny toes
into the sand.
The wind has snatched his yellow cap
and blows it far into the water as
Timmy moans and cries for Mother as
she recovers now the yellow blur.

His nose is running. Tears are welled.
Blond hair laughs as tho' it knows its plight—
no more cap until it dries.
And Timmy eats a hot dog filled
with sand, as four-year olds do.

Maybe when he's older he'll forget about this day,
I hope not.
Time takes care of youth,
and Timmy doesn't realize its fast escape.

A dog has found a Timmy friend and licks his face
and knocks him down upon the sand again
echoing sobs into the quiet afternoon.
"I'm sorry, Timmy, dogs don't know
their strength in love--"
and neither, I guess, do Timmys.

SHIRLEY SNEED

Voice like I never heard before. Oh, wow. It
was a good year, Shirley. Thanks.

Yesterday I saw you in the window.
It must have been very late,
    for the sun was nearly depleted.
And your reflection faded hard
    against the eve, and
    I nearly forgot
        your presence.
People saw from inside
    and watched me as tho'
    I were strange and curious.
You might have glared or made
    a funny face.
    You might have never left me
    standing there laughing
    except some dumb man ran into me, and
        I dropped my tennis shoes
        and realized then that you were gone.
I looked everywhere, but you were just
    vanished.
So, I just stood there feeling
    like an idiot,
    seeking some trace of you.
And then the children hollered
    far from down the street.

And there you were
     giving piggy-back rides
     in the grass, and
          surely, you looked
          like a child yourself
     and laughed as tho' the day had just
          begun.
I guess it comes as waves
     upon a mountain shore—
     slowly and readily.
So I decided
     to join your neurosis
     and chased you down the street
          screaming, yelling for a cop
          as tho' you'd stolen my tennis shoes.
And, Shirley Sneed, you big old creep,
     I ran into a
     trash can and nearly broke
          my shin bone.
At least there'll be a scar to
     remember well the day
          inside a barren park.
A child you appear to me—
     a delicacy so real and
          so potent.
A soul so intricate
     as the wing of a golden butterfly.
Maybe that is why
          I remember you so well—
     Maybe your beauty

        just stands out
          like something you see
        that takes your breath away
        and remains imbedded in your
            memory.
Nobody could understand
        it, Shirley,
        unless they met you the
            way I did,
              in a store window.

YARROW

One friend to come but once to me as though from no
one knows where—and one to save for a long, long time.

'Twas only 20 years
      A slender life a slender thread
      I heard the dreams of autumn
           shifting bove my head.

Who are you my yarrow?
      An empty dream, a dying gift.
      A rambler from the east
           Who's soon to sadly drift.

There is no love but that of time.
      And time takes time
      and I'm the cost.
Yarrow waits. Tomorrow waits.
      And I'll return.

Take me with you always
      to find the sun the starry day
      when friends are waiting for
           other years to slip away.

When I die, oh, yarrow
      I'll come at last into your own
      and watch you when you're sleeping
           and never find your face alone.

DAISY

What of this that promises the friends to new?
It comes a while and stays where the mind can
remember.

She gave me

a daisy and

asked if I

liked it.

How could

I tell her

how much

it meant?

So I ate it.

IT ALL BEGINS

*See the golden sunlight in my eyes? Maybe I
am worth something.*

. . . It all begins with friends
and has no
rhyme and no
finish.

Let it be as such
for now
and for a
long, long time . . .

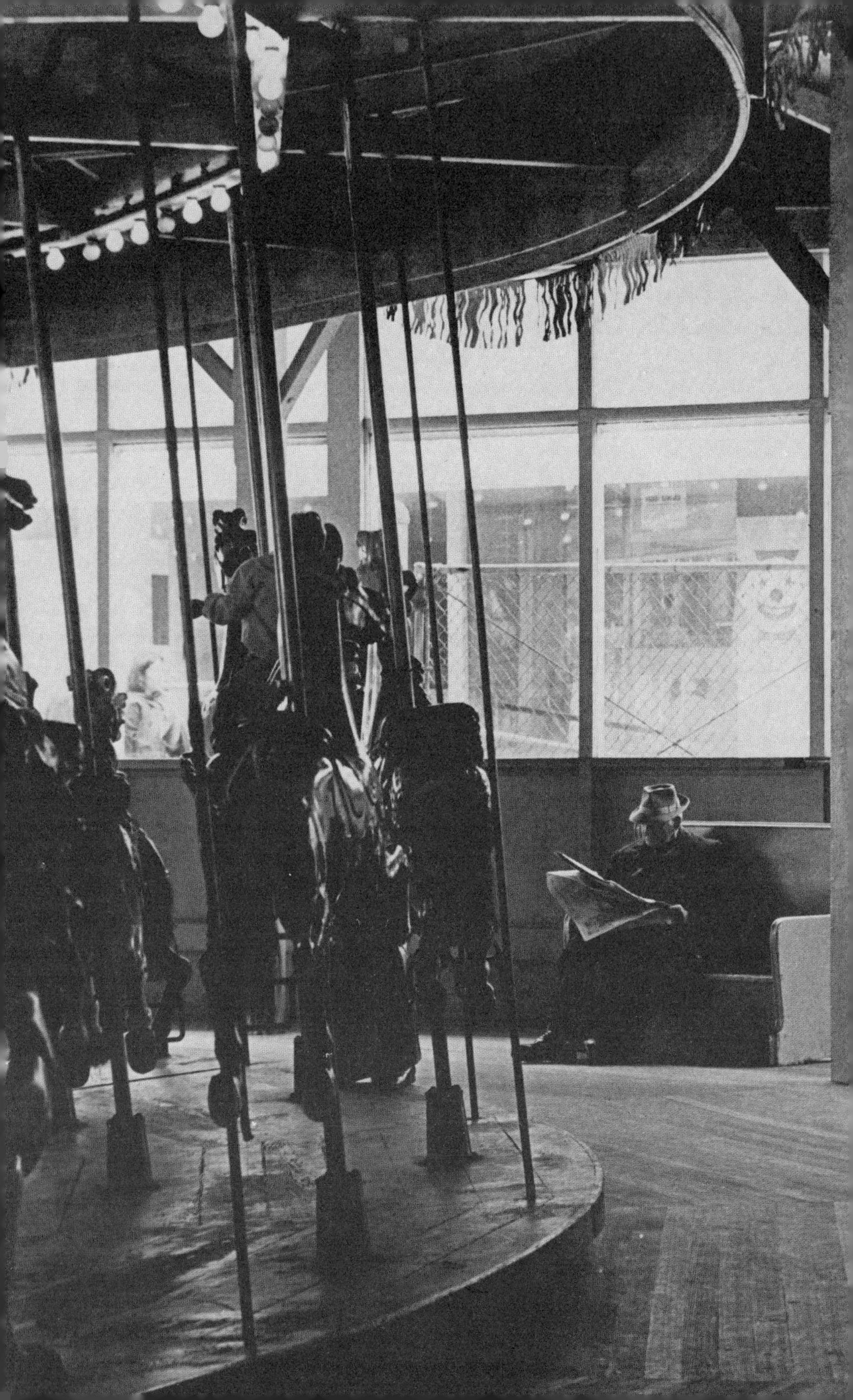

ALONENESS

Aloneness begins slowly-casting forth the lengthened shadow . . .
   asking me to stay awhile and listen to the change.
An old birch was downed last winter.
I sit upon its body's gravestone
   wondering if it knows my presence. . .
Being alone is just a time of seclusion,
   a time for introduction into my own soul,
   a time to search the dotted horizon
     and pick out tiny shapes and pieces.
They might belong to me one day — one day.
But then, when I am alone,
   I sense the newness of each second.
It vibrates as the highest pitch of crystal.
It brightens the already old existence
   of the season's somber face.
I try to make it smile. . .
A clown I am at times, throwing stones against the water;
   laughing out loud at my own foolish intentions.
I can never be lonely when I am alone.
How can there be an inch of loneliness in the crowded sky
   when you let go of a promise and reach for an uncertainty?
Forgive these lonely people who hide
   in empty corners and tilted bar stools.
They know not of a silent bliss.
They know of neither day nor night.
It all just flows together
   as watered ink upon a rain-fed street.
They are alone. They are lonely.
The two have clashed,
   yet they be partners at the same moment.
When they part, a body lies beneath the satin clouds
   and weeps for dreams that never even started.
So, I sit awhile longer as the world fades.
It enfolds me to its breast -- as if to have me stay.
Yet, I cannot. I may be lonely for other voices,
   but I shall never be lonely alone.

TEN ALONE

Ten be next to nothing when a dime is of pennies.
    Ten be mistaken, as marbles in the dirt.
But ten righteous others, whose sores thirsted of healing
    and relief, could only stumble into the front of Christ,
        as a bird against glass.
They grumble, their feet are bruised upon the outskirted road
    where none but the oxen walk.
They face no glory in this adjustment, as newborn flies
    to the steril wards of institutional demands.
They deprived their standard salvation of its arival
    by casting both the spear and the salt into another's breast.
Dejection be a stubborn fow,
    it clamps the links of every man against its own belt.
These ten are freed by their anguish,
    herding together in a pitiful claim of determination.
Where be these fossils?
They be sleeping in the gutters. . . wonded and boned.
They barely inhale, and clothing reeks of contamination.
Would it be best to hold a bonfire midst the modest classes,
    and burn these freaks before their children,
    as unwanted innards of swine and wolves?
Would it not be more a benevolent gesture than an act of
    violence?
Oh, we be such privileged judges
    with such moderate temptations. . . (or so we try to believe).
Should the murderers testify for the murderer?
Should the lepers place sentence on the leper?
I fear it should be so.
For our quick tongues do hibernate at challenge. . .
    and do attack at disgust or revenge.
Has the mind no brain? Only tongue? No sensitivity?
Does it only wish to see its blemishes destroyed
    and not healed?
We be of little joys. . . and selfish as the starving lion.
We bring no burden upon our outlines. . .
    so the ten are hidden in the brush till dark
    to scavenge the streets, filling their pockets
    with mildewed scraps.
The hour is up.
Christ is in the village,
    and ten lonely infections straggle to his view.

CHANGING MOON

The second moon has waned,
    it conveys a single foreshadow to my feet,
        almost as if drawn by my brief departure.
I have stood here before, when night was day,
        and day was but my closest comrade.
    You come at last in hesitation,
        weary, but not mistaken.
Night portrays its darkest cloak, becoming the
        sorcerer's assistant. . .
and it shares this art in quiet fulfillment, knowing that
    soon, your feet shall replace mine.
I bring with me an ivory strainer.
    It be ancient to these last hours,
        and its value will soon initiate your next duty.
Hold it with me before this full moon, and stand beneath
    its bent rays.
    This is where I matched my soul. I belong to this moon.
Its beams now filter out upon you, as do mine.
    All that I have is issued into your exquisitness. . .
        and what I am becomes you.
    With this parting, you shall not know of me,
        For I am gone to other promises,
    and these debts place new weights upon new shoulders.

I believe you are the only recipient to my fortitude.
None other could accept its power.
None other could unfold my true meanings.
    So many others await your new cause.

    Oh, that I could be with you at this venture's side.
That I could see the lanterns waiting in the
    peasant's windows.
That I could sit with you at their crudest tables,
    to share with you the barest essentials,
    and the most important.
That I could listen to you speak of my wisdom,
    and watch them weap for your incessant conclusions.
Oh, that I might bare witness to your interpretations. . .
    and follow you, to hold you when you weaken
        and shade you when you sleep.
We might have awakened the universe if we had tried together.
The spirit is so willing, yet the body is feeble.
    As much as I yearn to accompany you,

        other demands are pressing.
    And with this dawn, you shall be alone.

You are nearly full now. . . but your face is worried.
    No fear, my endless sister of today.
Only the earth awaits your new arrival.
    It summons to all regions of your essence.
Only the earth can listen.
If, in my death, I bring more life upon you,
    then all else is not vital. Only you.
    Only you withstand a struggled future, but it shall prove
        your most worthwhile task.
And, with this parting, I bid to you a fulfilling journey
    and a memory of what you represent.
I shall not for an instant leave your side. . . I shall be true to you
    until we meet beyond. And what you are, and what you will be
        shall divide and unite, and no stone shall be thrown.
Only kindness. So, go in peace, and take with you this ivory
    strainer, to entrust with another, if they be worthy, and
        only when your body is too feeble to support your mind.